phonics Adventures

Double Double Consonant Trouble

This book
belongs to:

_____

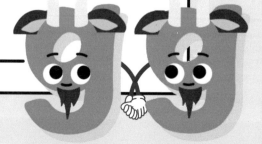

Check out our other adventures on our website:
https://phonicsadventures.my.canva.site/

Have ideas for Miss Jill's next great phonics journey? Reach out!
Instagram: @phonicsadventures
Email: phonicsadventures@gmail.com

Double, double, if it ends in just one,
With a short vowel sound, then a double is
done.

When adding -ing, -ed, or -er as an ending,
you see,
Double the consonant - it's that easy!

One-one-one, let's stick to that guide,
One vowel, one consonant, one syllable wide,
Use the doubling rule, side by side!

In the enchanting world of Alphabetia, nestled between rolling hills and whispering forests, there stood a school known as Letterland.

Here, the students weren't ordinary children, but living letters with curious minds, eager to discover their own role in the world of writing by improving their spelling so they could help children like you tell their stories.

One bright sunny morning, Miss Jill gathered her students beneath the branches of the Great Alphabet Tree.

"Today, my dear letters, we set off on a very important adventure," she announced, her eyes sparkling with excitement. "Our field trip will take us through the lands of Alphabetia to uncover the secrets of the Double Double Consonant Trouble!"

The letters cheered with delight,
excited to begin their adventure!

With a wave of her hand, the school bus approached, ready to take the letters on a journey to unravel their spelling errors for good.

The bus took them through shining rivers and over misty mountains,

past fields of blooming words, and forests of tangled sentences.
After a long day of travel...

they reached the Valley of Phonics, where the ancient Book of Rules lay hidden beneath a veil of mist.

As the letters approached, their hearts were pounding with anticipation. Miss Jill opened the book and began to read aloud, her voice echoing through the valley like music.

Double, double, if it ends in just one,

With a short vowel sound, then a double

is done.

When adding -ing, -ed, or -er as an

ending, you see,

Double the consonant - it's that easy!

One-one-one, let's stick to that guide,

One vowel, one consonant, one syllable

wide,

Use the doubling rule, side by side!

Examples:

bag + er = bagger

prefer + ed = preferred

grab + ing = grabbing

spot + ed = spotted

The letters gasped in awe, their eyes wide with wonder. They had found the answer they sought — the secret of the doubling rule!

The letters took off, exploring their new knowledge, and stumbled upon a sweet bunny.

The bunny seemed trapped in a state of hoping and hoping, yearning for a way to leap and bound instead.

"Double double consonant trouble!" cheered the letters in unison, and the once-hoping bunny found itself hopping.

No longer trapped hoping, it now bounced and hopped with joy, just as it was always meant to!

The now happy hopping bunny told the letters, "Hey, I have a friend that needs you, too!" The determined letters followed the bunny to meet his friend.

The bunny brought them to Woody the Woodpecker.

This sad woodpecker found himself in a predicament. Instead of tapping his beloved tree, he was trapped in a cycle of taping, trying to mend a crack.

He had gone through nearly a whole roll of tape and couldn't stop adding layers! But with the arrival of Miss Jill and her students, the letters of Alphabetia, came up with a solution...

With a chant of "double double consonant trouble," the magic surged, and Woody found himself tapping once more, the tape disappearing like mist in the morning sun. With renewed purpose, he tapped away, the forest echoing with the joyful rhythm, and his heart soaring with relief and gratitude.

Arriving back to the bus, ready to return to Letterland and head home to their uppercase parents, the little letters noticed that the bus driver, Mr. Redding, seemed horribly sad.

He could not stop moping. "What's wrong," asked little p, worried.

"Well, little p, someone spilled some water on the bus. This is no big deal, most of the time, but for some reason I can't stop moping to mop it up." Little p knew just the thing.

She said her special chant and helped turn Mr. Redding's moping to mopping! In no time, the bus was cleaned up and all the little letters loaded up to head back to Letterland.

From that day forth, the letters of Alphabetia lived and learned, guided by the wisdom of Miss Jill and the magic of their adventures.

And though they faced many challenges in the world of words, they knew that together, they could overcome anything.

Can you spy all of the double consonant words in this story?

trapped   stopped

bagger   tapping

jarred   tapped

grabbing   Redding

spotted   mopping

hopping

1-1-1 Doubling Rule

Double, double, if it ends in just one,
With a short vowel sound, then a double is done.

When adding -ing, -ed, or -er as an ending, you see,
Double the consonant - it's that easy!

One-one-one, let's stick to that guide,
One vowel, one consonant, one syllable wide,
Use the doubling rule, side by side!

When adding suffixes like -ing, -ed, or -er to a word, if the word ends with a single vowel followed by a single consonant, the consonant is doubled if the preceding vowel is short. This doubling ensures that the vowel remains short when the suffix is added, maintaining the word's pronunciation.

Exceptions:

If a word ends in silent -e but still has a short vowel, you can typically replace the e with a suffix without doubling the consonant!

(living, having, imaging)